Christmas Sparkle

Make your holiday décor twinkle with bright embellishments, from rhinestones to prairie points, appliqués, and more!

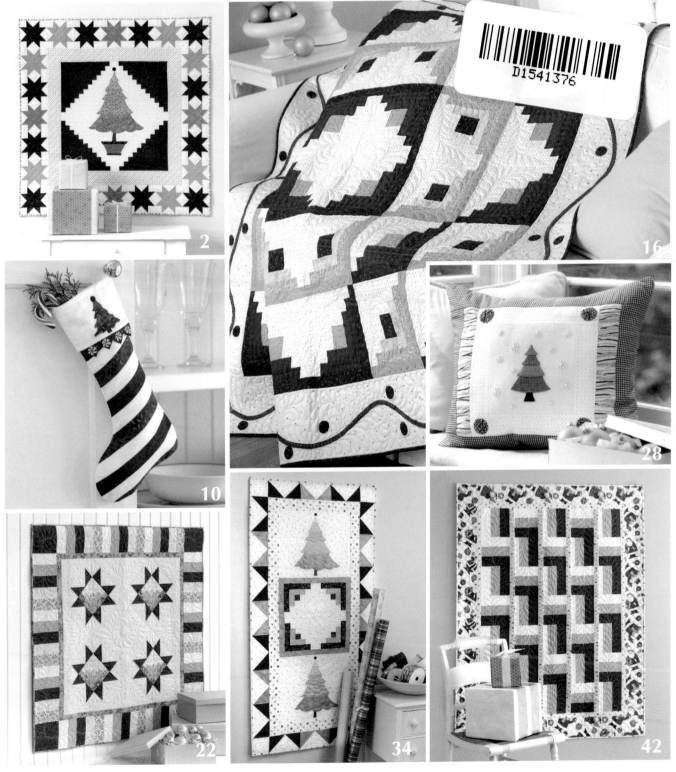

D1541376

LEISURE ARTS, INC. • Little Rock, Arkansas

STARRY CABINS

Finished Quilt Size: 43" x 43" (109 cm x 109 cm)
Finished Log Cabin Block Size: 12" x 12" (30 cm x 30 cm)
Finished Star Block Size: 6" x 6" (15 cm x 15 cm)

SHOPPING LIST

Yardage is based on 43"/44" (109 cm/112 cm) wide fabric with a usable width of 40" (102 cm). Fat quarters are approximately 22" x 18" (56 cm x 46 cm).

- ☐ 1¼ yds (1.1 m) of white tone-on-tone fabric for blocks
- ☐ 6 assorted green tone-on-tone fat quarters for blocks and trees
- ☐ 6 assorted red tone-on-tone fat quarters for blocks
- ☐ ½ yd (46 cm) of red dot fabric for inner border
- ☐ Scraps of brown, green, and red tone-on-tone fabrics for tree trunk and stand
- ☐ 2⅞ yds (2.6 m) of fabric for backing
- ☐ ⅜ yd (34 cm) of fabric for binding
- ☐ 51" x 51" (130 cm x 130 cm) piece of batting
- ☐ Hot fix rhinestones (we used 140 red 4 mm and 5 crystal 5 mm)
- ☐ Template plastic
- ☐ Removable fabric marking pen or pencil
- ☐ Hot fix rhinestone setting tool
- ☐ Fabric basting glue (optional)

CUTTING THE PIECES

*Follow **Rotary Cutting**, page 48, to cut fabric. Cut all strips from the selvage-to-selvage width of the fabric. Cut strips from fat quarters parallel to the long edge. Borders are cut exact length. All measurements include ¼" seam allowances.*

From white tone-on-tone fabric:
- Cut 5 strips 3½" wide. From these strips, cut 96 **rectangles** 2" x 3½".
- Cut 5 strips 2" wide. From these strips, cut 96 **small squares** 2" x 2".
- Cut 9 strips 1½" wide. From these strips:
  - Cut 4 **logs** 1½" x 1½" (#2).
  - Cut 4 **logs** 1½" x 2½" (#3).
  - Cut 4 **logs** 1½" x 3½" (#6).
  - Cut 4 **logs** 1½" x 4½" (#7).
  - Cut 4 **logs** 1½" x 5½" (#10).
  - Cut 4 **logs** 1½" x 6½" (#11).
  - Cut 4 **logs** 1½" x 7½" (#14).
  - Cut 4 **logs** 1½" x 8½" (#15).
  - Cut 4 **logs** 1½" x 9½" (#18).
  - Cut 4 **logs** 1½" x 10½" (#19).
  - Cut 4 **logs** 1½" x 11½" (#22).
  - Cut 4 **logs** 1½" x 12½" (#23).

From *each* of 3 green tone-on-tone fat quarters:
- Cut 4 **large squares** 3½" x 3½".
- Cut 32 **small squares** 2" x 2".

Continued on page 4.

Starry Cabins continued.

From red tone-on-tone fat quarter #1:
• Cut 4 **logs** 1$\frac{1}{2}$" x 1$\frac{1}{2}$" (#1).

From red tone-on-tone fat quarter #2:
• Cut 4 **logs** 1$\frac{1}{2}$" x 2$\frac{1}{2}$" (#4).
• Cut 4 **logs** 1$\frac{1}{2}$" x 3$\frac{1}{2}$" (#5).

From red tone-on-tone fat quarter #3:
• Cut 4 **logs** 1$\frac{1}{2}$" x 4$\frac{1}{2}$" (#8).
• Cut 4 **logs** 1$\frac{1}{2}$" x 5$\frac{1}{2}$" (#9).

From red tone-on-tone fat quarter #4:
• Cut 4 **logs** 1$\frac{1}{2}$" x 6$\frac{1}{2}$" (#12).
• Cut 4 **logs** 1$\frac{1}{2}$" x 7$\frac{1}{2}$" (#13).

From red tone-on-tone fat quarter #5:
• Cut 4 **logs** 1$\frac{1}{2}$" x 8$\frac{1}{2}$" (#16).
• Cut 4 **logs** 1$\frac{1}{2}$" x 9$\frac{1}{2}$" (#17).

From red tone-on-tone fat quarter #6:
• Cut 4 **logs** 1$\frac{1}{2}$" x 10$\frac{1}{2}$" (#20).
• Cut 4 **logs** 1$\frac{1}{2}$" x 11$\frac{1}{2}$" (#21).

From *each* of 3 red tone-on-tone fat quarters:
• Cut 4 **large squares** 3$\frac{1}{2}$" x 3$\frac{1}{2}$".
• Cut 32 **small squares** 2" x 2".

From red dot fabric:
• Cut 2 **side inner borders** 3$\frac{1}{2}$" x 24$\frac{1}{2}$".
• Cut 2 **top/bottom borders** 3$\frac{1}{2}$" x 30$\frac{1}{2}$".

From fabric for binding:
• Cut 5 **binding strips** 2$\frac{1}{4}$" wide.

CUTTING THE APPLIQUÉS

Use patterns, pages 8-9, and follow **Making And Using Templates**, page 49, to cut appliqués.

From assorted green tone-on-tone fat quarters:
• Cut 1 of each **tree section A-E**.

From scraps of brown, green, and red print fabrics:
• Cut 1 **trunk**.
• Cut 1 **stand**.
• Cut 1 **upper trim**.
• Cut 1 **lower trim**.
• Cut 1 **topper**.

MAKING THE BLOCKS

*Follow **Machine Piecing**, page 50, and **Pressing**, page 51, to make quilt top. Use $\frac{1}{4}$" seam allowances throughout.*

Log Cabin Block
*For **each** Log Cabin Block you will need: From white tone-on-tone, 1 of **each** log #2, #3, #6, #7, #10, #11, #14, #15, #18, #19, #22, and #23. From red tone-on-tone, 1 of **each** log #1, #4, #5, #8, #9, #12, #13, #16, #17, #20, and #21.*

1.   Sew #1 and #2 **logs** together to make **Unit 1**.

Unit 1

2.   Sew 1 #3 **log** to Unit 1 to make **Unit 2**.

Unit 2

3.   Sew 1 #4 **log** to Unit 2 to make **Unit 3**.

Unit 3

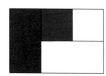

4.   Sew 1 #5 **log** to Unit 3 to make **Unit 4**.

Unit 4

5. Referring to **Log Cabin Block Diagram**, continue working in numerical order to add logs #6-#23 to make **Log Cabin Block**. Make 4 Log Cabin Blocks.

Log Cabin Block (make 4)

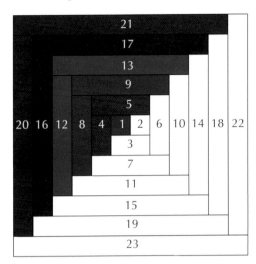

Star Block

For **each** Star Block you will need, 4 white rectangles, 4 white small squares, 1 green or red large square and 8 matching small squares.

1. Draw a diagonal line on wrong side of **each** red or green **small square**.

2. Place 1 marked square on one end of 1 **rectangle**. Stitch on drawn line **(Fig. 1)**. Trim ¼" from stitching line. Open up and press, pressing seam allowances to darker fabric **(Fig. 2)**.

Fig. 1

Fig. 2

3. Repeat Step 2 to add 1 marked square to the opposite end of rectangle to make **Flying Geese Unit**. Make 4 Flying Geese Units.

Flying Geese Unit (make 4)

4. Sew 1 Flying Geese Unit to opposite sides of a **large square** to make **Unit 5**.

Unit 5

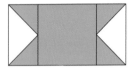

5. Sew 1 white small square to each end of a Flying Geese Unit to make **Unit 6**. Make 2 Unit 6's.

Unit 6 (make 2)

6. Sew Unit 5 and Unit 6's together to make **Star Block**. Repeat Steps 1-5 to make 24 (12 red and 12 green) Star Blocks.

Star Block (make 24)

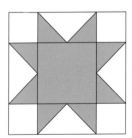

ASSEMBLING THE QUILT TOP

*Refer to **Quilt Top Diagram** to assemble the quilt top.*

1. Sew 2 Log Cabin Blocks together to make a **Row**. Make 2 Rows.

Row (make 2)

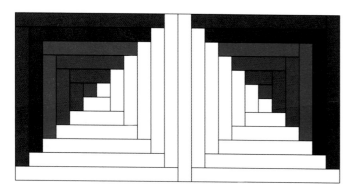

2. Sew Rows together to make **Quilt Top Center**.
3. Working from the background up, center **trunk**, **stand**, **upper trim**, **lower trim**, 1 of each **tree section A-E**, and 1 **topper** on Quilt Top Center. Pin or use basting glue to temporarily hold appliqués in place.
4. Follow **Needle-Turn Appliqué**, page 51, to blindstitch appliqués to Quilt Top Center.

5. Matching centers and corners, sew 1 **side inner border** to each side of the Quilt Top Center. Sew **top/bottom inner borders** to Quilt Top Center.
6. Alternating red and green stars, sew 5 Star Blocks together to make **Side Star Border**. Make 2 Side Star Borders. Sew 1 **Side Star Border** to each side of the Quilt Top Center.
7. Using 7 Star Blocks, repeat Step 6 to make and sew **Top/Bottom Star Borders** to quilt top.

COMPLETING THE QUILT

1. Follow **Quilting**, page 53, to mark, layer, and quilt as desired. Quilt shown is machine quilted with three rows of echo quilting around the tree and meandering quilting in the remainder of the white background. There is a corner feather quilted in each red corner. The inner border and star centers are crosshatch quilted. There is curved outline quilting on and around the star points.
2. Follow **Adding a Hanging Sleeve**, page 55, if a hanging sleeve is desired.
3. Use **binding strips** and follow **Binding**, page 56, to bind quilt.
4. Follow manufacturer's instructions to add red and crystal rhinestones to tree and stand.

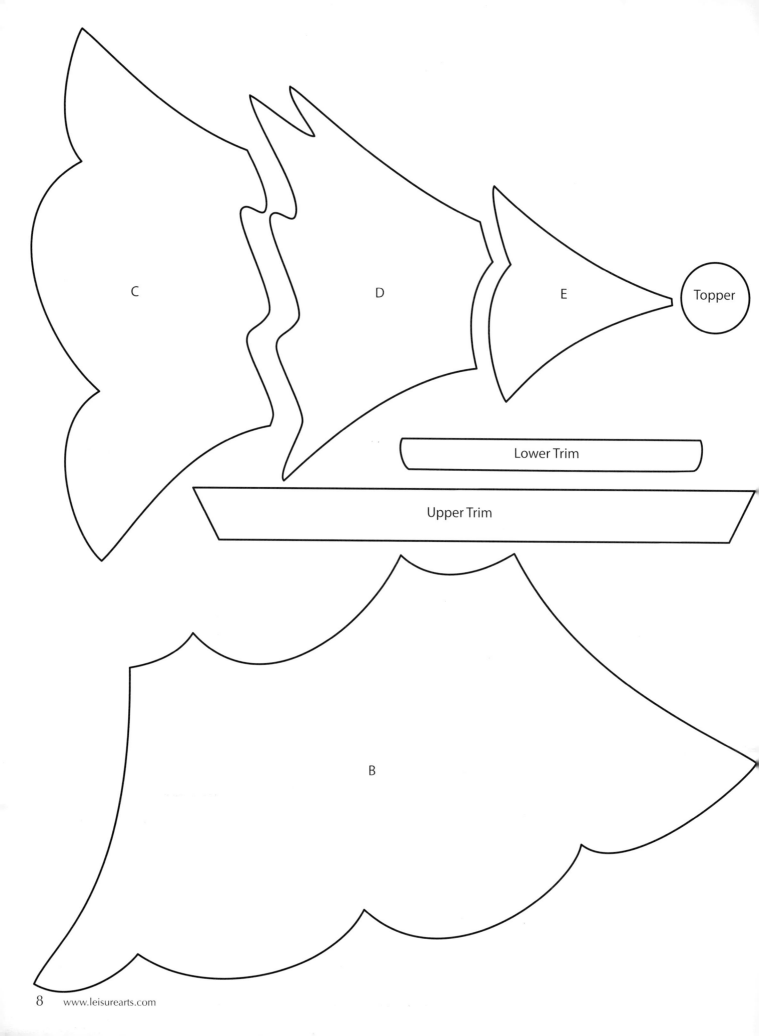

C

D

E

Topper

Lower Trim

Upper Trim

B

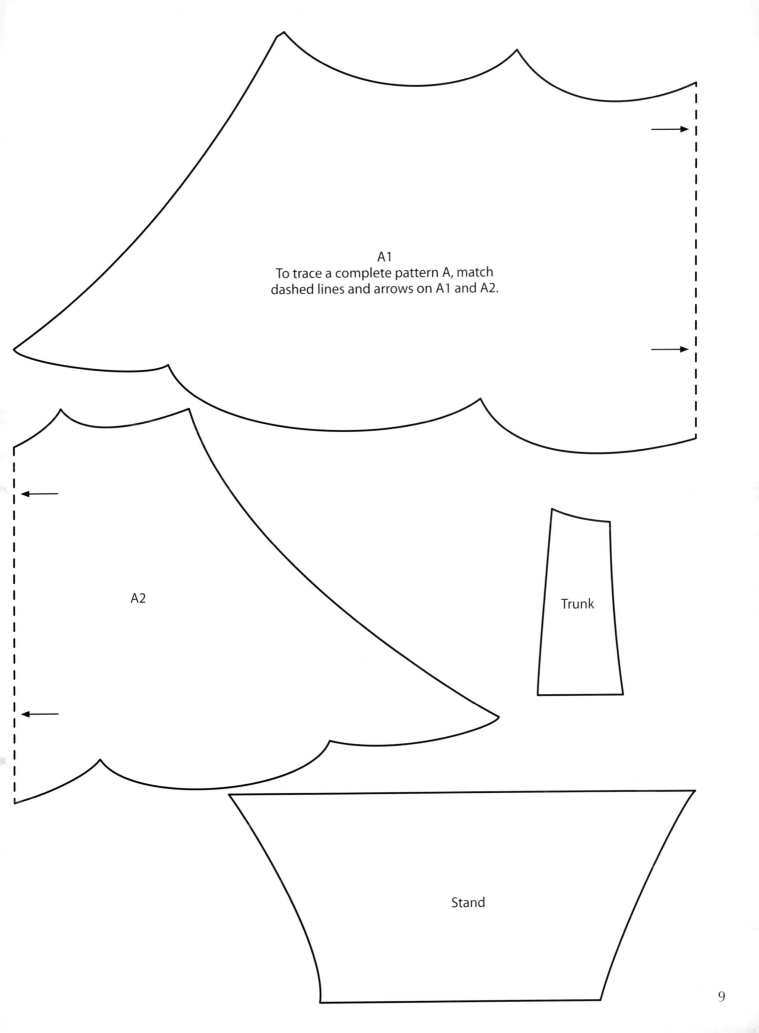

A1
To trace a complete pattern A, match
dashed lines and arrows on A1 and A2.

A2

Trunk

Stand

CHRISTMAS STOCKING

Finished Size: approximately 7¼" x 14¼" (18 cm x 36 cm)

SHOPPING LIST

Yardage is based on 43"/44" (109 cm/112 cm) wide fabric with a usable width of 40" (102 cm). Fat quarters are approximately 22" x 18" (56 cm x 46 cm).

- ☐ 1⅛ yds (1 m) of white tone-on-tone fabric
- ☐ 1 fat quarter *each* of 1 green and 1 red tone-on-tone fabric
- ☐ 12" x 12" (30 cm x 30 cm) square of novelty print fabric with small [approx. ½"- ⅝" (13 mm-16 mm) dia.] motifs
- ☐ Scrap of brown fabric
- ☐ Template plastic
- ☐ Tracing paper
- ☐ Removable fabric marking pen or pencil

CUTTING THE PIECES

*Follow **Rotary Cutting**, page 48, to cut fabric. Cut all strips from the selvage-to-selvage width of the fabric. Cut strips from fat quarters parallel to the long edge. Follow **Making And Using Templates**, page 49, to cut **squares**. All measurements include ¼" seam allowances.*

From white tone-on-tone fabric:
- Cut 2 strips 14" wide. From these strips, cut 1 **stocking back**, 1 **lining front**, and 1 **lining back** *each* 14" x 17½".
- Cut 5 strips 1½" wide. From these strips, cut 8 **small strips** 1½" x 14" and 1 **binding strip** 1¼" x 13".
- Cut 1 **cuff front**, 1 **cuff back**, 1 **cuff front lining**, and 1 **cuff back lining** using cuff pattern, page 14.
- Cut 1 **hanger strip** 1" x 3".

From green fat quarter:
- Cut 5 **small strips** 1½" x 14".

From red fat quarter:
- Cut 4 **small strips** 1½" x 14".

From novelty print:
- Cut 4 **squares** using template, page 15.

CUTTING THE APPLIQUÉS
*Use patterns, pages 14-15, and follow **Making And Using Templates**, page 49, to cut appliqués.*

From green tone-on-tone fat quarter:
- Cut 1 of each **tree section A-D**.

From red tone-on-tone fat quarter:
- Cut 1 **topper**.

From scrap of brown fabric:
- Cut 1 **trunk**.

Continued on page 12.

Christmas Stocking continued.

MAKING THE STOCKING

*Follow **Machine Piecing**, page 50, and **Pressing**, page 51, to make the stocking. Use ¹/₄" seam allowances throughout.*

1. Sew 8 white, 4 red, and 5 green **small strips** together to make **Unit 1**.

Unit 1

2. Trace **stocking**, pages 14-15, onto tracing paper; cut out pattern on drawn line.

3. **Note:** *The angle at which the pattern is placed on the stocking back determines the angle of the stripes on the front. For horizontal stripes, place the pattern completely vertical. For diagonal stripes, place the stocking diagonally.* Angling as desired, center and pin pattern on wrong side of stocking back (**Fig. 1**); draw around pattern with fabric marker. **Do not** cut out stocking.

Fig. 1

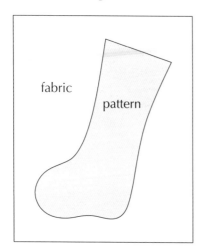

4. Use pattern to draw 1 stocking on lining back.

5. Matching right sides and raw edges, layer stocking back and Unit 1; pin. Leaving top edge open, sew on drawn line (**Fig. 2**).

Fig. 2

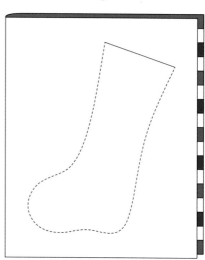

6. Cutting on drawn line across the top and leaving a ¹/₄" seam allowance around stitching, cut out **stocking**. Clip curves up to but not through stitching; press. Turn stocking to the right side (**Fig. 3**); press.

Fig. 3

7. Repeat Steps 5-6 using lining back and lining front to make **lining**. Do not turn right side out.

8. Place lining inside stocking, making sure foot is pushed in completely, side seams align, and top raw edges are even. Baste raw edges together.

COMPLETING THE STOCKING

Follow Needle-Turn Appliqué, page 51, to add the appliqués.

1. With the wider edge at the top, work from the background up to appliqué **trunk**, **tree sections A-D**, and **topper** to the center of **cuff front**.

2. Matching right sides, sew cuff front and **cuff back** together along each side to make **cuff**. Turn cuff to the right side *(Fig. 4)*; press. Repeat for **cuff front lining** and **cuff back lining** to make **cuff lining**.

Fig. 4

3. For the prairie points, fold 1 **square** in half twice diagonally *(Figs. 5-6)*. Make 4 **Prairie Points**.

Fig. 5

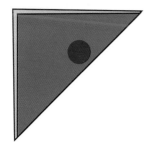

Fig. 6

4. With motifs facing down and tucking points inside adjacent points, align raw edges of Prairie Points with bottom edge of cuff front *(Fig. 7)*. Baste Prairie Points in place.

Fig. 7

5. Matching right sides, side seams, and raw edges, slip cuff inside cuff lining; pin. Sew bottom edge of cuff and lining together. Turn cuff right side out. Prairie Points should be facing down; press *(Fig. 8)*.

Fig. 8

6. With right sides facing out, slip cuff over stocking *(Fig. 9)*. Match raw edges and side seams; baste around top edge.

Fig. 9

7. For binding, press 1 long edge of binding strip ¼" to the wrong side. Matching right sides and raw edges, pin binding strip around top edge of stocking. Mark binding where ends meet *(Fig. 10)*; unpin. Sew ends together along mark forming a loop. Leaving a ¼" seam allowance, trim ends.

Fig. 10

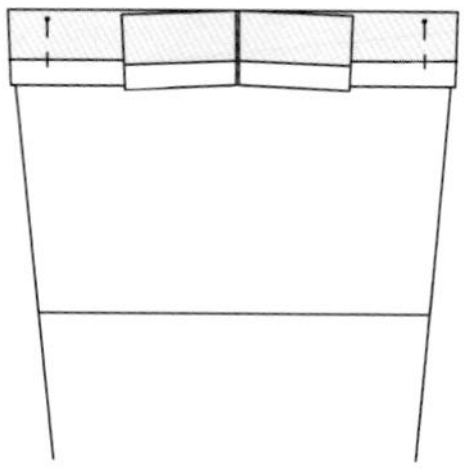

8. Matching right sides and raw edges, pin loop to top of stocking. Sew binding around top of stocking. Fold binding over to the lining side of stocking and Blindstitch, page 58, in place.

9. For hanger, press all 4 edges of **hanger strip** ¼" to the wrong side. Fold strip in half lengthwise. Topstitch close to long folded edge. Pin ends of hanger to inside and outside of stocking at side seam. Stitch across ends through all layers just below binding *(Fig. 11)*.

Fig. 11

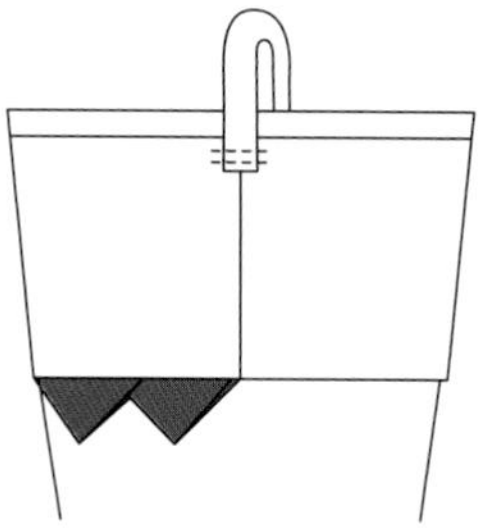

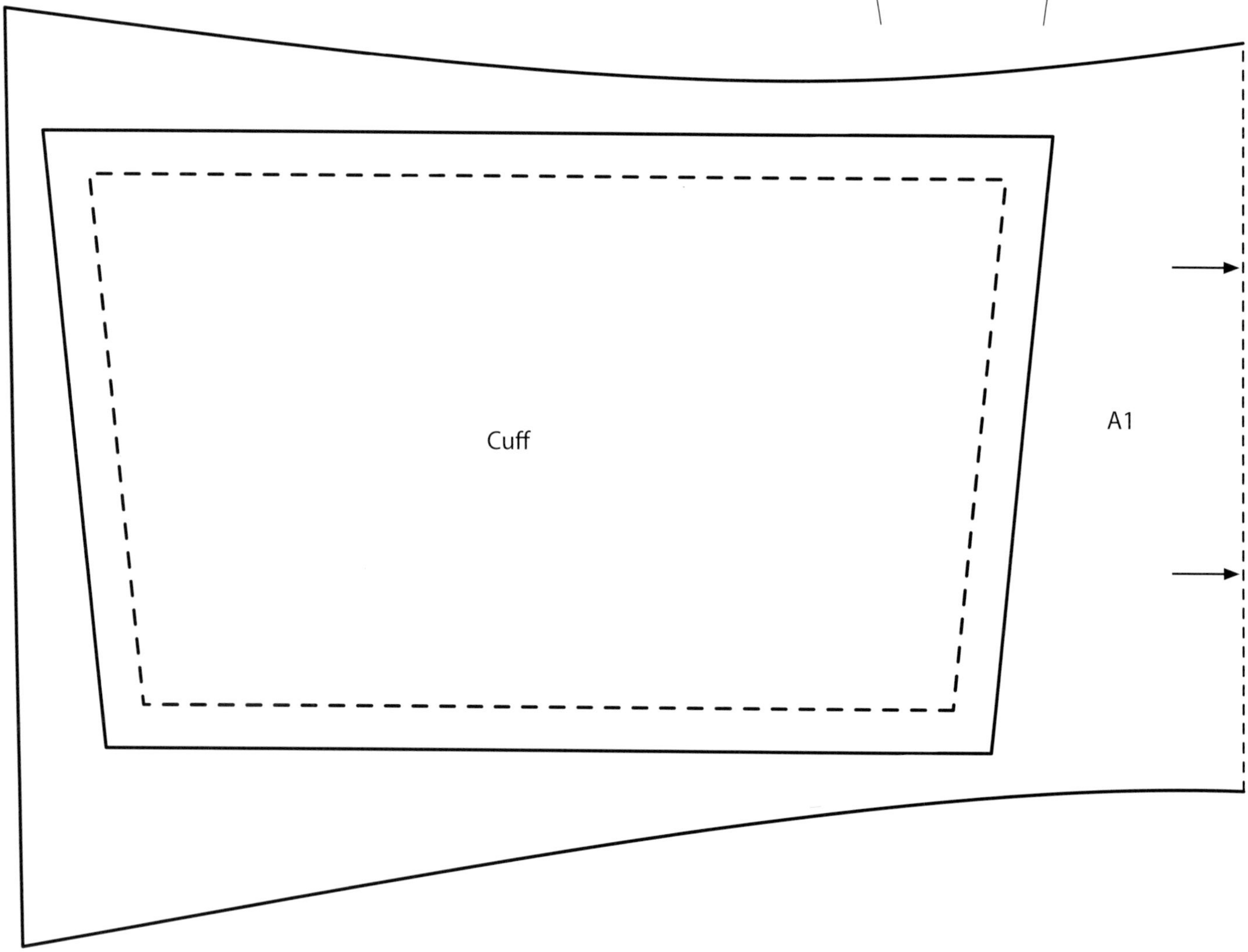

Cuff

A1

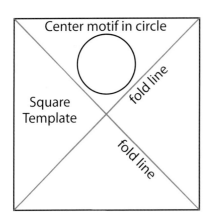

Center motif in circle

Square Template

fold line

fold line

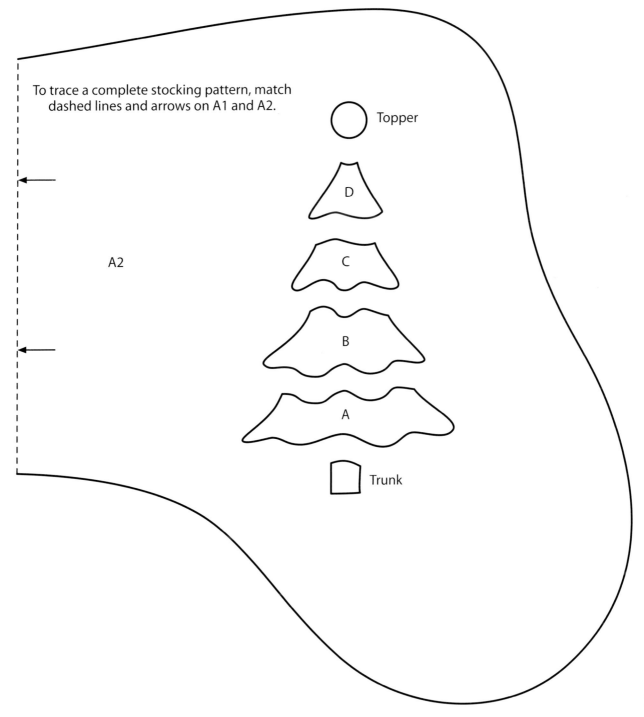

To trace a complete stocking pattern, match dashed lines and arrows on A1 and A2.

Topper

A2

D

C

B

A

Trunk

15

HOLLY LOG CABIN

Finished Quilt Size: 61" x 61" (155 cm x 155 cm)
Finished Block Size: 8" x 8" (20 cm x 20 cm)

SHOPPING LIST

Yardage is based on 43"/44" (109 cm/112 cm) wide fabric with a usable width of 40" (102 cm). Fat quarters are approximately 22" x 18" (56 cm x 46 cm).

☐ 1$\frac{7}{8}$ yds (1.7 m) of cream dot fabric #1 for border
☐ 1$\frac{1}{2}$ yds (1.4 m) of cream dot fabric #2 for blocks
☐ $\frac{1}{4}$ yd (23 cm) of green print fabric #1 for blocks
☐ $\frac{1}{4}$ yd (23 cm) of green print fabric #2 for blocks
☐ $\frac{5}{8}$ yd (57 cm) of green print fabric #3 for blocks
☐ $\frac{1}{2}$ yd (46 cm) of green print fabric #4 for vine
☐ $\frac{1}{8}$ yd (11 cm) of green print fabric #5 for holly leaves
☐ $\frac{3}{8}$ yd (34 cm) of red print fabric #1 for blocks and circles
☐ $\frac{1}{2}$ yd (46 cm) of red print fabric #2 for blocks and circles
☐ $\frac{1}{2}$ yd (46 cm) of red print fabric #3 for blocks and circles
☐ $\frac{1}{2}$ yd (46 cm) of fabric for binding
☐ 3$\frac{7}{8}$ yds (3.5 m) of fabric for backing
☐ 69" x 69" (175 cm x 175 cm) piece of batting
☐ $\frac{1}{2}$" (12 mm) wide bias tape maker
☐ Template plastic
☐ Removable fabric marking pen or pencil
☐ Fabric basting glue

CUTTING THE PIECES

*Follow **Rotary Cutting**, page 48, to cut fabric. Cut all strips from the selvage-to-selvage width of the fabric. Borders are cut exact length. All measurements include $\frac{1}{4}$" seam allowances.*

From cream dot fabric #1:
• Cut 2 *lengthwise* side borders 6$\frac{1}{2}$" x 48$\frac{1}{2}$".
• Cut 2 *lengthwise* top/bottom borders 6$\frac{1}{2}$" x 60$\frac{1}{2}$".

From cream dot fabric #2:
• Cut 32 strips 1$\frac{1}{2}$" wide. From these strips:
  • Cut 36 **logs** 1$\frac{1}{2}$" x 2$\frac{1}{2}$" (#2).
  • Cut 36 **logs** 1$\frac{1}{2}$" x 3$\frac{1}{2}$" (#3).
  • Cut 36 **logs** 1$\frac{1}{2}$" x 4$\frac{1}{2}$" (#6).
  • Cut 36 **logs** 1$\frac{1}{2}$" x 5$\frac{1}{2}$" (#7).
  • Cut 36 **logs** 1$\frac{1}{2}$" x 6$\frac{1}{2}$" (#10).
  • Cut 36 **logs** 1$\frac{1}{2}$" x 7$\frac{1}{2}$" (#11).

From green print fabric #1:
• Cut 4 strips 1$\frac{1}{2}$" wide. From these strips:
  • Cut 16 **logs** 1$\frac{1}{2}$" x 3$\frac{1}{2}$" (#4).
  • Cut 16 **logs** 1$\frac{1}{2}$" x 4$\frac{1}{2}$" (#5).

From green print fabric #2:
• Cut 5 strips 1$\frac{1}{2}$" wide. From these strips:
  • Cut 16 **logs** 1$\frac{1}{2}$" x 5$\frac{1}{2}$" (#8).
  • Cut 16 **logs** 1$\frac{1}{2}$" x 6$\frac{1}{2}$" (#9).

Continued on page 18.

Holly Log Cabin continued.

From green print fabric #3:
- Cut 2 strips 2½" wide. From these strips, cut 20 **logs** 2½" x 2½" (#1).
- Cut 8 strips 1½" wide. From these strips:
  - Cut 16 **logs** 1½" x 7½" (#12).
  - Cut 16 **logs** 1½" x 8½" (#13).

From green print fabric #4:
- Cut 1 **vine square** 17" x 17".

From red print fabric #1:
- Cut 1 strip 2½" wide. From this strip, cut 16 **logs** 2½" x 2½" (#1).
- Cut 4 strips 1½" wide. From these strips:
  - Cut 20 **logs** 1½" x 3½" (#4).
  - Cut 20 **logs** 1½" x 4½" (#5).

From red print fabric #2:
- Cut 7 strips 1½" wide. From these strips:
  - Cut 20 **logs** 1½" x 5½" (#8).
  - Cut 20 **logs** 1½" x 6½" (#9).

From red print fabric #3:
- Cut 9 strips 1½" wide. From these strips:
  - Cut 20 **logs** 1½" x 7½" (#12).
  - Cut 20 **logs** 1½" x 8½" (#13).

From fabric for binding:
- Cut 7 **binding strips** 2¼" wide.

CUTTING THE APPLIQUÉS
*Use patterns, page 20, and follow **Making And Using Templates**, page 49, to cut appliqués.*

From green print #5:
- Cut 8 **leaves**.

From red prints #1, #2, and #3:
- Cut a *total* of 44 **circles**.

MAKING THE BLOCKS
*Follow **Machine Piecing**, page 50, and **Pressing**, page 51, to make the quilt top. Use ¼" seam allowances throughout.*

Block A
*For **each** Block A you will need: From red print #1, 1 log #1, From cream dot #2, 1 of **each** log #2, #3, #6, #7, #10, and #11. From green prints, 1 of **each** log #4, #5, #8, #9, #12, and #13.*

1. Sew #1 and #2 **logs** together make **Unit 1**.

Unit 1

2. Sew 1 #3 **log** to Unit 1 to make **Unit 2**.

Unit 2

3. Sew 1 #4 **log** to Unit 2 to make **Unit 3**.

Unit 3

4. Sew 1 #5 **log** to Unit 3 to make **Unit 4**.

Unit 4

5. Referring to **Block A Diagram**, continue working in numerical order to add logs #6-#13 to Unit 4 to make **Block A**. Make 16 Block A's.

Block A (make 16)

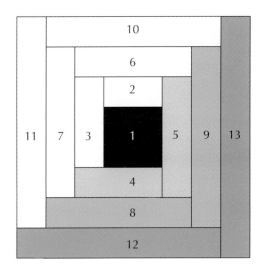

Block B

*For **each** Block B you will need: From green print #3, 1 log #1. From cream dot #2, 1 of **each** log #2, #3, #6, #7, #10, and #11. From red prints, 1 of **each** log #4, #5, #8, #9, #12, and #13.*

1. Repeat Steps 1-5 using green logs, cream dot logs, and red print logs to make 20 Block B's.

Block B (make 20)

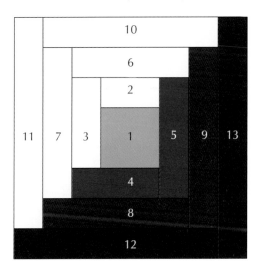

ASSEMBLING THE QUILT TOP

*Refer to **photo**, page 21, to assemble the quilt top.*

1. Sew 2 Block A's and 4 Block B's together to make **Row 1**. Make 4 Row 1's.

Row 1 (make 4)

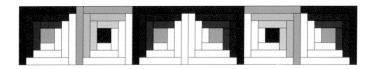

2. Sew 4 Block A's and 2 Block B's together to make **Row 2**. Make 2 Row 2's.

Row 2 (make 2)

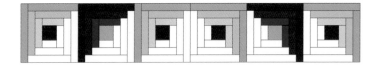

3. Sew Rows together to make **Quilt Top Center**.

Quilt Top Center

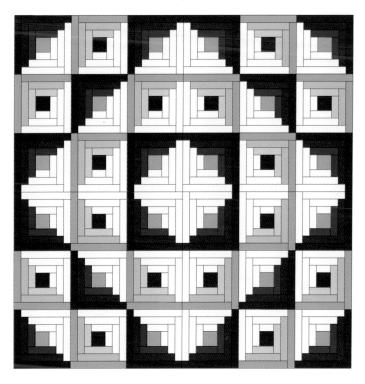

4. Matching centers and corners, sew 1 **side border** to each side of the Quilt Top Center. Repeat to sew **top/bottom borders** to the Quilt Top Center.

ADDING THE APPLIQUÉS

1. Using **vine square**, follow **Making A Continuous Bias Strip**, page 52, to make a 1" wide, 240" long bias strip.
2. Follow manufacturer's instructions to use bias tape maker to make bias tape from bias strip. Cut bias tape into four 60" **vines**.
3. Using basting glue to temporarily hold vines in place, arrange 1 vine on each border. Blindstitch, page 58, vines in place.
4. Arrange 1 leaf over each vine end. Follow **Needle-Turn Appliqué**, page 51, to stitch leaves in place.
5. To make berries, turn the edge of each **circle** ¹/₄" to the wrong side and make a running stitch around the edge with 2 strands of thread *(Fig. 1)*. Pull threads tight from both ends and tie a knot; clip threads and flatten berries *(Fig. 2)*.

6. Using basting glue to temporarily hold berries in place, arrange berries on border. Blindstitch berries in place.

COMPLETING THE QUILT

1. Follow **Quilting**, page 53, to mark, layer, and quilt as desired. Quilt shown is machine quilted with L-shaped feathers in opposite corners of each block. There is in the ditch quilting between the border and quilt top center and feathers along each side of the vines.
2. Follow **Adding a Hanging Sleeve**, page 55, if a hanging sleeve is desired.
3. Use **binding strips** and follow **Binding**, page 56, to bind quilt.

Fig. 1

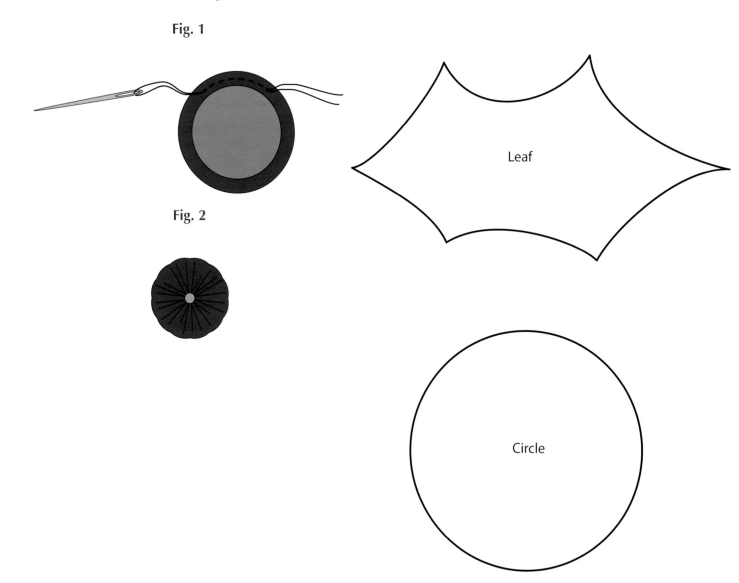

Fig. 2

Leaf

Circle

NORTH STAR LOG CABIN

Finished Quilt Size: 41" x 41" (104 cm x 104 cm)
Finished Block Size: 10" x 10" (25 cm x 25 cm)

SHOPPING LIST

Yardage is based on 43"/44" (109 cm/112 cm) wide fabric with a usable width of 40" (102 cm).

☐ 1⅛ yds (1 m) of cream dot fabric for blocks and background

☐ ¼ yd (23 cm) of cream mini dot fabric for outer border

☐ ⅜ yd (34 cm) of cream/green print fabric for blocks and outer border

☐ ¼ yd (23 cm) of green print #1 fabric for blocks and outer border

☐ ⅜ yd (34 cm) of green print #2 fabric for blocks and outer border

☐ ⅜ yd (34 cm) of green print #3 fabric for blocks and inner border

☐ ¾ yd (69 cm) of dark green print fabric for star points and outer border

☐ 2¾ yds (2.5 m) of fabric for backing

☐ ⅜ yd (34 cm) of fabric for binding

☐ 49" x 49" (124 cm x 124 cm) piece of batting

CUTTING THE PIECES

*Follow **Rotary Cutting**, page 48, to cut fabric. Cut all strips from the selvage-to-selvage width of the fabric. Inner borders are cut exact length. All measurements include ¼" seam allowances.*

From cream dot fabric:

• Cut 4 strips 3" wide. From these strips, cut 16 **rectangles** 3" x 5½" and 16 **squares** 3" x 3".

• Cut 1 strip 8" wide. From this strip, cut 2 squares 8" x 8". Cut each square in half *once* diagonally to make 4 **corner triangles.**

• Cut 1 strip 15½" wide. From this strip, cut 1 square 15½" x 15½". Cut square in half *twice* diagonally to make 4 **side triangles.**
From the remainder of this strip,
  • Cut 1 **center square** 10½" x 10½".

From cream mini dot fabric:

• Cut 3 strips 2½" wide. From these strips, cut 6 **border rectangles** 2½" x 14".

From cream/green print fabric:

• Cut 3 strips 2½" wide. From these strips, cut 6 **border rectangles** 2½" x 14".

• Cut 2 strips 1½" wide. From these strips:
  • Cut 4 **logs** 1½" x 1½" (#2).
  • Cut 4 **logs** 1½" x 2½" (#3).
  • Cut 4 **logs** 1½" x 3½" (#6).
  • Cut 4 **logs** 1½" x 4½" (#7).

From green print fabric #1:

• Cut 3 strips 2½" wide. From these strips, cut 6 **border rectangles** 2½" x 14".

• Cut 4 **logs** 1½" x 1½" (#1).

From green print fabric #2:

• Cut 3 strips 2½" wide. From these strips, cut 6 **border rectangles** 2½" x 14".

• Cut 1 strip 1½" wide. From this strip:
  • Cut 4 **logs** 1½" x 2½" (#4).
  • Cut 4 **logs** 1½" x 3½" (#5).

Continued on page 24.

North Star Log Cabin continued.

From green print fabric #3:
- Cut 2 **side inner borders** 1³/₈" x 28³/₄".
- Cut 2 **top/bottom inner borders** 1³/₈" x 30¹/₂".
- Cut 1 strip 1¹/₂" wide. From this strip:
  - Cut 4 **logs** 1¹/₂" x 4¹/₂" (#8).
  - Cut 4 **logs** 1¹/₂" x 5¹/₂" (#9).

From dark green print fabric:
- Cut 3 strips 2¹/₂" wide. From these strips, cut 6 **border rectangles** 2¹/₂" x 14".
- Cut 1 strip 5¹/₂" wide. From this strip, cut 4 **corner squares** 5¹/₂" x 5¹/₂".
- Cut 3 strips 3" wide. From these strips, cut 32 **squares** 3" x 3".

From fabric for binding:
- Cut 5 **binding strips** 2¹/₄" wide.

MAKING THE BLOCKS

*Follow **Machine Piecing**, page 50, and **Pressing**, page 51, to make the quilt top. Use ¹/₄" seam allowances throughout.*

*For **each** Block you will need: From cream/green print, 1 of **each** log #2, #3, #6, and #7. From green print, 1 of **each** log #1, #4, #5, #8, and #9.*

1. Sew #1 and #2 **logs** together to make **Unit 1**.

Unit 1

2. Sew 1 #3 **log** to Unit 1 to make **Unit 2**.

Unit 2

3. Sew 1 #4 **log** to Unit 2 to make **Unit 3**.

Unit 3

4. Sew 1 #5 **log** to Unit 3 to make **Unit 4**.

Unit 4

5. Referring to **Block Center Diagram**, continue working in numerical order to add logs #6-#9 to Unit 4 to make **Block Center**. Make 4 Block Centers.

Block Center (make 4)

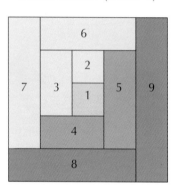

6. Draw a diagonal line on wrong side of *each* dark green **square**.
7. Place 1 marked square on one end of 1 **rectangle**. Stitch on drawn line *(Fig. 1)*. Trim ¹/₄" from stitching line. Open up and press seam allowances to darker fabric *(Fig. 2)*.

Fig. 1   **Fig. 2**

8. Repeat Step 7 to add 1 marked square to the opposite end of rectangle to make **Flying Geese Unit**. Make 16 Flying Geese Units.

Flying Geese Unit (make 16)

9. Sew 1 Flying Geese Unit to opposite sides of a Block Center to make **Unit 5**. Make 4 Unit 5's.

Unit 5 (make 4)

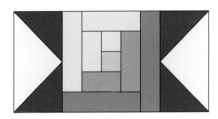

10. Sew 1 cream dot **square** to each end of 1 Flying Geese Unit to make **Unit 6**. Make 8 Unit 6's.

Unit 6 (make 8)

11. Sew 1 Unit 6 to each remaining side of 1 Unit 5 to make **Star Block**. Make 4 Star Blocks.

Star Block (make 4)

ASSEMBLING THE QUILT TOP

*Refer to **Quilt Top Diagram**, page 27, to assemble the quilt top.*

1. Referring to **Assembly Diagram**, arrange **corner triangles**, **setting triangles**, Star Blocks, and **center square** into diagonal Rows.

Assembly Diagram

2. Sew Rows together to make **Quilt Top Center**. Square Quilt Top Center to $28^3/_4$"x $28^3/_4$".
3. Matching centers and corners, sew 1 **side inner border** to opposite sides of the Quilt Top Center. Repeat to add **top/bottom inner borders**.

25

4. Arranging fabrics as desired, match long edges and sew 15 **border rectangles** together to make **Unit 7**. Make 2 identical Unit 7's.

Unit 7 (make 2)

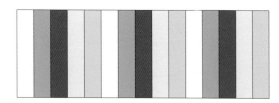

5. Cut each Unit 7 in half lengthwise. Trim each Unit 7 to 5½" x 30½" to make 4 **outer borders**.

Outer Border (make 4)

6. Sew 1 outer border to each side of the Quilt Top Center.
7. Sew 1 **corner square** to each end of each remaining outer border *(Fig. 3)*. Sew outer borders to remaining sides of **Quilt Top**.

Fig. 3

COMPLETING THE QUILT

1. Follow **Quilting**, page 53, to mark, layer, and quilt as desired. Quilt shown is machine quilted with a feather wreath in the center square. There are corner feathers in the setting and corner triangles. The Star Blocks are outline quilted and have feathers in the cream backgrounds. There is a feather design in the borders.
2. Follow **Adding a Hanging Sleeve**, page 55, if a hanging sleeve is desired.
3. Use **binding strips** and follow **Binding**, page 56, to bind quilt.

CHRISTMAS TREE PILLOW

Finished Size: 22" x 18" (56 cm x 46 cm)

SHOPPING LIST

Yardage is based on 43"/44" (109 cm/112 cm) wide fabric with a usable width of 40" (102 cm).

☐ 1$1/8$ yds (1 m) of red gingham fabric
☐ $1/8$ yd (11 m) of red/green/cream stripe fabric
☐ $1/4$ yd (23 cm) of cream dot fabric
☐ 8$1/2$" x 8$1/2$" (22 cm x 22 cm) square of cream wool fabric
☐ 6" x 6" (15 cm x 15 cm) square **each** of 2 green wool fabrics
☐ Scrap of brown wool fabric
☐ 22$1/2$" x 18$1/2$" (57 cm x 47 cm) rectangle of thin cotton batting
☐ 12 assorted small and medium snowflake buttons with shanks removed
☐ Embroidery floss - green and brown
☐ Tracing paper
☐ Paper-backed fusible web
☐ Gem-Tac™ Embellishing Glue
☐ Polyester fiberfill

CUTTING THE PIECES

*Follow **Rotary Cutting**, page 48, to cut fabric. Cut all strips from the selvage-to-selvage width of the fabric. Borders are cut exact length. All measurements include $1/4$" seam allowances.*

From red gingham fabric:
• Cut 2 **side outer borders** 3$1/2$" x 12$1/2$".
• Cut 2 **top/bottom outer borders** 3$1/2$" x 22$1/2$".
• Cut 1 **pillow back** 22$1/2$" x 18$1/2$".

From red/green/cream stripe fabric:
• Cut 2 **ruffle strips** 2$1/2$" x 20".

From cream dot fabric:
• Cut 2 **side inner borders** 2$1/2$" x 8$1/2$".
• Cut 2 **top/bottom inner borders** 2$1/2$" x 12$1/2$".

CUTTING THE APPLIQUÉS

*Follow **Preparing Fusible Appliqués**, page 50, to use patterns, page 33.*

From red gingham fabric:
• Cut 4 **circles**.

From green wool fabrics:
• Cut **tree sections A** and **C** from 1 square.
• Cut **tree sections B** and **D** from remaining square.

From scrap of brown wool fabric:
• Cut 1 **trunk**.

MAKING THE PILLOW TOP

*Follow **Machine Piecing**, page 50, and **Pressing**, page 51, to make the pillow top. Use $1/4$" seam allowances throughout.*

1. Remove paper backing from appliqué pieces.
2. Working from background up, arrange **trunk** and **tree sections A-D** in center of cream wool **square**; fuse.

Continued on page 30.

Christmas Tree Pillow continued.

3. Making stitches about ⅛" long and ⅛" apart, make **Straight Stitches** *(Fig. 1)*, over the edges of each appliqué with 3 strands of matching floss *(Fig. 2)*.

Fig. 1

Fig. 2

4. Matching centers and corners, sew **side inner borders** to opposite sides of wool square. Repeat to add **top/bottom inner borders** to make **Unit 1**.

Unit 1

5. Sew 2 lines of basting stitches, ⅛" apart, close to each long edge of 1 **ruffle strip** *(Fig. 3)*. Repeat for remaining ruffle strip.

Fig. 3

6. To gather ruffle strip, pull bobbin threads only *(Fig. 4)* until **ruffle** measures 12½". Make 2 ruffles.

Fig. 4

7. Sew 1 **ruffle** to each side of Unit 1 to make **Unit 2**.

Unit 2

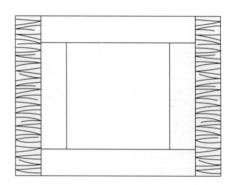

8. Matching centers and corners, sew **side outer borders** to opposite sides of Unit 2. Repeat to add **top/bottom outer borders** to make **Unit 3**.

Unit 3

9. To make yo-yo's, turn the edge of each **circle** ¹/₄" to the wrong side and make Running Stitches around the edge with 2 strands of thread *(Fig. 5)*. Pull threads tight from both ends and tie a knot; clip threads *(Fig. 6)*.

Fig. 5

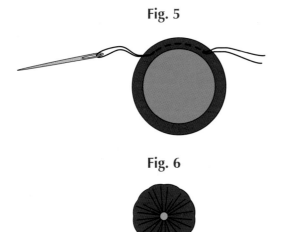

Fig. 6

10. Arrange yo-yo's on inner border corners; pin. Blindstitch, page 58, yo-yo's in place to complete **Pillow Top.**

Pillow Top

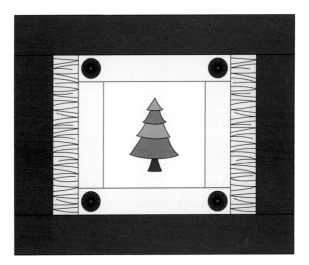

ASSEMBLING THE PILLOW

1. To round the pillow corners, draw a diagonal line on wrong side of **pillow back** across *each* corner as shown in *Fig. 7*.

Fig. 7

Tip: Rounded corners are easier to stuff with fiberfill, making a nicer looking pillow.

2. Matching raw edges, layer batting rectangle, pillow top (right side up) and pillow back (right side down); pin.
3. Beginning and ending off the fabric edge and leaving a 6" opening along bottom edge, sew around pillow being sure to sew on drawn line at corners *(Fig. 8)*.

Fig. 8

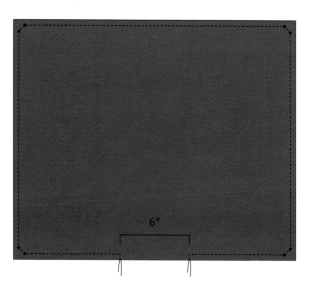

Tip: Stitching off the fabric edge on either side of an opening makes it easier to turn the seam allowance inward when sewing the opening closed.

4. Clip corners and turn pillow right side out; press.
5. Stuff pillow firmly with fiberfill. Hand sew opening closed.
6. Glue snowflakes to pillow front.

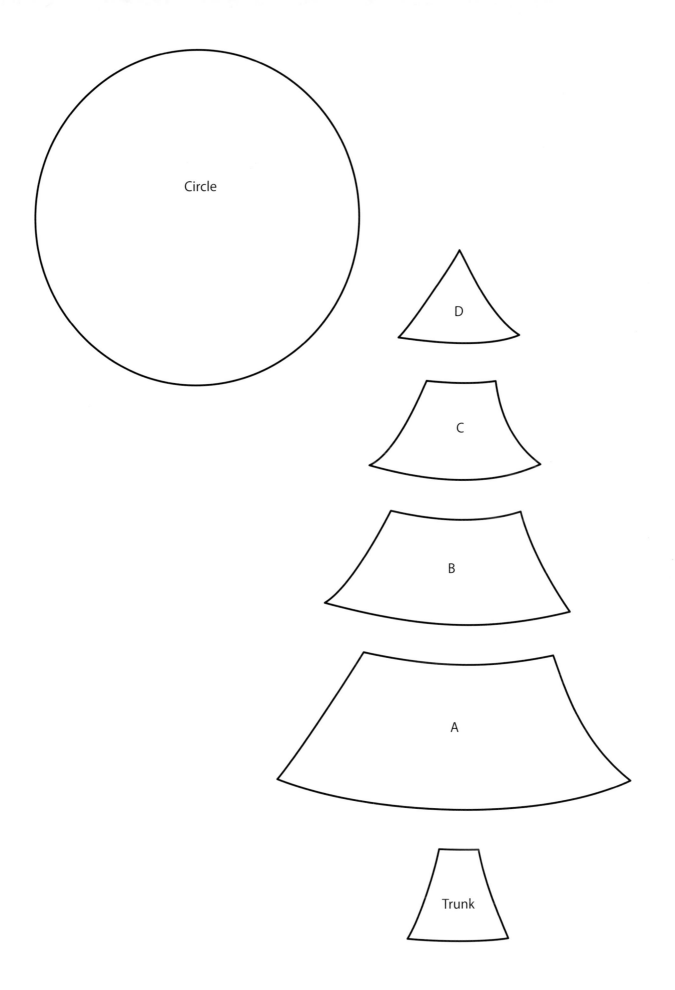

Circle

D

C

B

A

Trunk

TREES IN THE CABIN

Finished Quilt Size: 25" x 49" (64 cm x 124 cm)
Finished Block Size: 14" x 14" (36 cm x 36 cm)

This quilt offers you the option of making a wall hanging or a table runner simply by reversing the direction of one Tree Block as you construct the quilt top.

SHOPPING LIST

Yardage is based on 43"/44" (109 cm/112 cm) wide fabric with a usable width of 40" (102 cm).

☐ 1⅛ yds (1 m) of cream small dot fabric for blocks and outer border
☐ ¼ yd (23 cm) of cream large dot fabric for inner border
☐ ⅛ yd (11 cm) of red print fabric #1 for blocks and outer border
☐ ⅜ yd (34 cm) of red print fabric #2 for blocks
☐ ⅛ yd (11 cm) of green stripe fabric for blocks and appliqués
☐ ⅜ yd (34 cm) of green print fabric for blocks, outer border, and appliqués
☐ Scraps of 1 red, 1 brown, and 3 assorted green print fabrics for appliqués
☐ 1⅝ yds (1.5 m) of fabric for backing
☐ ⅜ yd (34 cm) of fabric for binding
☐ 33" x 57" (84 cm x 145 cm) piece of batting
☐ Crystal 5 mm hot fix rhinestones (we used 13)
☐ Hot fix rhinestone setting tool
☐ Template plastic
☐ Fabric basting glue (optional)

CUTTING THE PIECES

*Follow **Rotary Cutting**, page 48 to cut fabric. Cut all strips from the selvage-to-selvage width of the fabric. Inner borders are cut exact length. All measurements include ¼" seam allowances.*

From cream small dot fabric:
- Cut 1 strip 12½" wide. From this strip, cut 2 **background rectangles** 12½" x 14½".
- Cut 3 strips 4" wide. From these strips, cut 20 **squares** 4" x 4".
- Cut 1 strip 3½" wide. From this strip, cut 4 **corner squares** 3½" x 3½".
- Cut 3 strips 1½" wide. From these strips:
  - Cut 4 **logs** 1½" x 1½" (#2).
  - Cut 4 **logs** 1½" x 2½" (#3).
  - Cut 4 **logs** 1½" x 3½" (#6).
  - Cut 4 **logs** 1½" x 4½" (#7).
  - Cut 4 **logs** 1½" x 5½" (#10).
  - Cut 4 **logs** 1½" x 6½" (#11).

From cream large dot fabric:
- Cut 2 **side inner borders** 2½" x 38½".
- Cut 2 **top/bottom inner borders** 2½" x 18½".

From red print fabric #1:
- Cut 4 **logs** 1½" x 1½" (#1).
- Cut 4 **logs** 1½" x 4½" (#8).
- Cut 4 **logs** 1½" x 5½" (#9).

From red print fabric #2:
- Cut 12 **squares** 4" x 4".

Continued on page 36.

Trees In The Cabin continued.

From green stripe fabric:
• Cut 4 **logs** 1¹⁄₂" x 2¹⁄₂" (#4).
• Cut 4 **logs** 1¹⁄₂" x 3¹⁄₂" (#5).

From green print fabric:
• Cut 1 strip 4" wide. From this strip, cut 8 **squares** 4" x 4".
• Cut 4 **logs** 1¹⁄₂" x 6¹⁄₂" (#12).
• Cut 4 **logs** 1¹⁄₂" x 7¹⁄₂" (#13).

From fabric for binding:
• Cut 5 **binding strips** 2¹⁄₄" wide.

CUTTING THE APPLIQUÉS
Use patterns, page 41, and follow Making And Using Templates, page 49, to cut appliqués.

From scraps of red, brown, and green print fabrics:
• Cut 2 of *each* tree section **B**, **D**, and **E**.
• Cut 2 **toppers**.
• Cut 2 **trunks**.

From green print fabric:
• Cut 2 **tree sections A**.

From green stripe fabric:
• Cut 2 **tree sections C**.

MAKING THE BLOCK
Follow Machine Piecing, page 50, and Pressing, page 51, to make the quilt top. Use ¹⁄₄" seam allowances throughout.

Log Cabin Block
*For **each** Unit 5 you will need: From cream small dot, 1 of **each** log #2, #3, #6, #7, #10, and #11. From green stripe, 1 of **each** log #4 and #5. From green print, 1 of **each** log #12 and #13. From red print #1, 1 of **each** log #1, #8, and #9.*

1. Sew #1 and #2 **logs** together make **Unit 1**.

Unit 1

2. Sew 1 #3 **log** to Unit 1 to make **Unit 2**.

Unit 2

3. Sew 1 #4 **log** to Unit 2 to make **Unit 3**.

Unit 3

4. Sew 1 #5 **log** to Unit 3 to make **Unit 4**.

Unit 4

5. Continue working in numerical order to add **logs** #6-#13 to Unit 4 to make **Unit 5**. Make 4 Unit 5's.

Unit 5 (make 4)

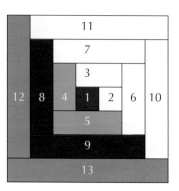

6. Sew 4 Unit 5's together to make **Log Cabin Block**.

Log Cabin Block

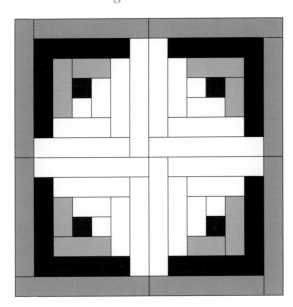

Tree Blocks

1. Position long edges of 1 **background rectangle** horizontally. Working from the background up, center 1 **trunk**, 1 of each **tree section A-E**, and 1 **topper** on rectangle. Pin or use basting glue to temporarily hold appliqués in place.

2. Follow **Needle-Turn Appliqué**, page 51, to Blindstitch, page 58, appliqués to background rectangle to make **Tree Block**. Make 2 Tree Blocks.

Tree Block (make 2)

ASSEMBLING THE QUILT TOP

*Refer to **Quilt Top Diagram**, page 39, to assemble the quilt top.*

1. Sew 1 Tree Block to opposite sides of Log Cabin Block to make **Unit 6**. ***Note:*** *To make a **wall hanging**, Tree Blocks should face the same direction. For a **table runner**, Tree Blocks should face opposite directions.*

Unit 6 (Wall Hanging)   Unit 6 (Table Runner)

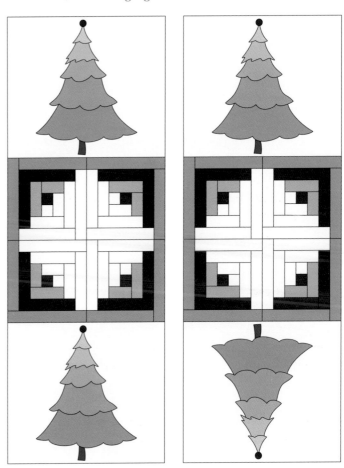

2. Matching centers and corners, sew 1 **side inner border** to each long edge of Unit 6. Repeat to add **top/bottom borders** to short edges to make **Quilt Top Center**.

3. Draw a diagonal line on wrong side of *each* cream **square**.

4. With right sides together, place 1 marked square on top of 1 red **square**. Stitch seam ¼" from each side of drawn line *(Fig. 1)*.

Fig. 1

5. Cut apart on drawn line. Open up and press seam allowances to darker fabric to make 2 **Triangle-Square A's**. Trim Triangle-Square A's to 3½" x 3½". Make 24 Triangle- Square A's.

Triangle-Square A (make 24)

6. Using cream and green **large squares,** repeat Steps 4-5 to make 16 **Triangle-Square B's**.

Triangle-Square B (make 16)

7. Sew 8 Triangle-Square A's and 6 Triangle-Square B's together to make **side outer border**. Make 2 side outer borders.

Side Outer Border (make 2)

8. Sew side outer borders to Quilt Top Center.

9. Sew 4 Triangle-Square A's, 2 Triangle-Square B's, and 2 **corner squares** together to make **top/bottom outer border**. Make 2 top/bottom outer borders.

Top/bottom Outer Border (make 2)

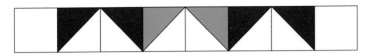

10. Sew top/bottom outer borders to Quilt Top Center to complete **Quilt Top**.

COMPLETING THE QUILT

1. Follow **Quilting**, page 53, to mark, layer, and quilt as desired. Quilt shown is machine quilted with a snowflake in the center of the Log Cabin Block and is stipple quilted across the remainder of the block. The backgrounds of the Tree Blocks are stipple quilted. The inner border has a loop and star design and the outer border has stipple quilting in the cream triangles and curved outline quilting in the red and green triangles.

2. Follow **Adding a Hanging Sleeve**, page 55, if a hanging sleeve is desired.

3. Use **binding strips** and follow **Binding**, page 56, to bind quilt.

4. Follow manufacturer's instructions to attach the **crystals** to the quilted snowflake.

Quilt Top Diagram

Topper

E

D

C

B

A

Trunk

RUFFLED SPLIT RAIL FENCE

Finished Quilt Size: 41" x 53" (104 cm x 135 cm)
Finished Block Size: 6" x 6" (15 cm x 15 cm)

SHOPPING LIST

Yardage is based on 43"/44" (109 cm/112 cm) wide fabric with a usable width of 40" (102 cm).

- ☐ 1³/₈ yds (1.3 m) of Christmas print fabric for outer border
- ☐ ⁷/₈ yd (80 cm) of cream dot fabric for ruffles and inner border
- ☐ ¹/₂ yd (46 cm) **each** of cream, green, and red tone-on-tone fabrics for blocks
- ☐ 3¹/₂ yds (3.2 m) of fabric for backing
- ☐ ¹/₂ yd (46 cm) of fabric for binding
- ☐ 49" x 61" (124 cm x 155 cm) piece of batting
- ☐ Ruffler sewing machine foot (optional)*

*Ruffles can be made by using a sewing machine basting stitch and pulling the thread to gather the fabric **or** by using a special ruffler sewing machine foot.

CUTTING THE PIECES

*Follow **Rotary Cutting**, page 48, to cut fabric. Cut all strips from the selvage-to-selvage width of the fabric. Borders are cut exact length. All measurements include ¹/₄" seam allowances.*

From Christmas print fabric:
- Cut 2 *lengthwise* **side outer borders** 4¹/₂" x 44¹/₂".
- Cut 2 *lengthwise* **top/bottom outer borders** 4¹/₂" x 40¹/₂".

From cream dot fabric:
- Cut 2 **side inner borders** 1¹/₂" x 42¹/₂", piecing as necessary.
- Cut 2 **top/bottom inner borders** 1¹/₂" x 32¹/₂".
- Cut 8 **ruffle strips** 2¹/₂" wide.

From *each* cream, green, and red tone-on-tone fabric:
- Cut 6 **strips** 2¹/₂" wide.

From fabric for binding:
- Cut 6 **binding strips** 2¹/₄" wide.

MAKING THE BLOCKS

*Follow **Machine Piecing**, page 50, and **Pressing**, page 51, to make the quilt top. Use ¹/₄" seam allowances throughout.*

1. Matching long edges, sew 1 cream, 1 green, and 1 red **strip** together to make **Strip Set**. Make 6 Strip Sets.

Strip Set (make 6)

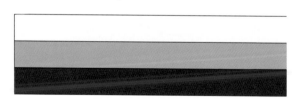

Continued on page 44.

Ruffled Split Rail Fence continued.

2. Cut across each Strip Set at 6¹/₂" intervals **(Fig. 1)** to make **Block**. Make 35 Blocks.

Fig. 1

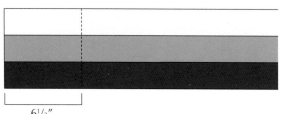

6¹/₂"

Block (make 35)

ASSEMBLING THE QUILT TOP

*Refer to **Assembly Diagram**, page 46, to assemble the quilt top. Follow either Method 1 **or** Method 2, below, to make the ruffles.*

Method 1: Using Basting Stitches

1. Matching short ends, sew 2 **ruffle strips** together with a diagonal seam **(Fig. 2)**.

(Fig. 2)

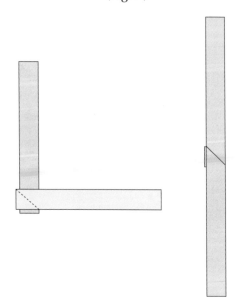

2. Matching wrong sides and raw edges, press ruffle strip in half lengthwise. Sew 2 lines of basting stitches, ¹/₈" apart, inside the ¹/₄" seam allowance **(Fig. 3)**.

(Fig. 3)

3. To gather strip, pull the 2 bobbin threads, only, **(Fig. 4)** until the **ruffle** measures 42¹/₂".

(Fig. 4)

4. Repeat Steps 1-4 to make 4 ruffles.

Method 2: Using A Ruffler Foot

1. Referring to **Fig. 2**, sew **ruffle strips** together end to end with a diagonal seam to make a **continuous strip**.
2. Matching wrong sides and raw edges, press continuous strip in half lengthwise.
3. Attach ruffler foot. Using the continuous strip, follow the manufacturer's instructions to make a **ruffle**. *Note: Ruffle shown was stitched with 6 stitches between ruffles and a medium ruffle depth.*
4. Cut ruffle into four 42¹/₂" lengths.

Quilt Top Assembly

1. Referring to **Assembly Diagram**, page 46, for block orientation, sew 7 Blocks together to make *vertical* **Row 1**. Repeat to make **Rows 3** and **5**.
2. Sew 7 Blocks together to make *vertical* **Row 2**. Repeat to make **Row 4**.
3. Matching raw edges, baste 1 ruffle to the left edges of Rows 2-5 (*Fig. 5*).
4. Sew Rows together to make **Quilt Top Center.**
5. Matching centers and corners, sew **side inner borders** to Quilt Top Center. Repeat to add **top/bottom inner borders.**
6. Repeat Step 5 to sew **side,** then **top/bottom outer borders** to Quilt Top Center.

Fig. 5

Rows 2 & 4   Rows 3 & 5

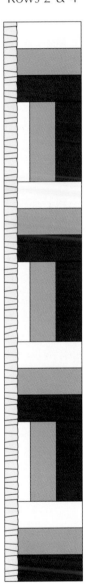 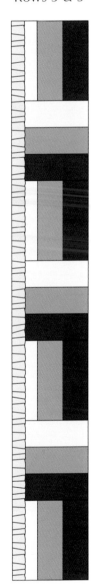

COMPLETING THE QUILT

1. Follow **Quilting**, page 53, to mark, layer, and quilt as desired. Quilt shown is machine quilted with a continuous vertical feather in each Row. The inner border is outline quilted and the outer border is crosshatch quilted.

2. Follow **Adding a Hanging Sleeve**, page 55, if a hanging sleeve is desired.

3. Use **binding strips** and follow **Binding**, page 56, to bind quilt.

Assembly Diagram

Row 1   Row 2   Row 3   Row 4   Row 5

47

GENERAL INSTRUCTIONS

To make your quilting easier and more enjoyable, we encourage you to carefully read all of the general instructions, study the Figs. and photographs, and familiarize yourself with the individual project instructions before beginning a project.

FABRICS

SELECTING FABRICS

Choose high-quality, medium-weight 100% cotton fabrics. All-cotton fabrics hold a crease better, fray less, and are easier to quilt than cotton/polyester blends.

Yardage requirements listed for each project are based on 43"/44" wide fabric with a "usable" width of 40" after shrinkage and trimming selvages. Actual usable width will probably vary slightly from fabric to fabric. Our recommended yardage lengths should be adequate for occasional re-squaring of fabric when many cuts are required.

PREPARING FABRICS

Pre-washing fabrics may cause edges to ravel. As a result, your pre-cut fabric pieces such as fat quarters or scraps may not be large enough to cut all of the pieces required for your chosen project. Therefore, we do not recommend pre-washing your yardage or pre-cut fabrics. Refer to **Caring For Your Quilt**, page 59, for instructions on washing your finished quilt.

Before cutting, prepare fabrics with a steam iron set on cotton and starch or sizing. The starch or sizing will give the fabric a crisp finish. This will make cutting more accurate and may make piecing easier.

After preparing, leave fat quarters flat. Fold yardage lengthwise with wrong sides together and matching selvages.

ROTARY CUTTING

• Place fabric on work surface with fold closest to you.

• Cut all strips from the selvage-to-selvage width of the fabric unless otherwise indicated in project instructions.

• Square left edge of fabric using rotary cutter and rulers *(Figs. 1-2)*.

Fig. 1

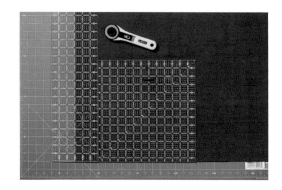

Fig. 2

- To cut each strip required for a project, place ruler over cut edge of fabric, aligning desired marking on ruler with cut edge; make cut *(Fig. 3)*.

Fig. 3

- When cutting several strips from a single piece of fabric, it is important to make sure that cuts remain at a perfect right angle to the fold; square fabric as needed.

MAKING AND USING TEMPLATES

Our patterns for the circles and the square templates (pages 15, 20, and 33) include seam allowances. Patterns for the appliqué templates do not include seam allowances.

1. To make a template from a pattern, use a permanent fine-point pen to carefully trace solid lines of pattern onto template plastic. Trace over any additional markings. Cut out template along inner edge of drawn line. Check template against original pattern for accuracy.
2. If using the **square** template, place template on the **right** side of the fabric with traced circle centered over desired motif. Use a sharp fabric-marking pencil to draw around template. Cut out fabric piece using scissors or rotary cutting tools.
3. If using a **circle** template, place template on the **right** side of the fabric. Use a sharp fabric-marking pencil to draw around template. Cut out fabric piece along drawn line using scissors.
4. If using an **appliqué** template, place template on the **right** side of the appliqué fabric. Lightly draw around template with pencil, leaving at least 1" between shapes. Repeat for number of shapes specified in project instructions. Cut out shapes approximately ³/₁₆" outside drawn line. Clip inside curves and points to but not through drawn line.

PREPARING FUSIBLE APPLIQUÉS

1. Place paper-backed fusible web, paper side up, over appliqué pattern. Trace pattern onto paper side of web with pencil as many times as indicated in project instructions for a single fabric.
2. Follow manufacturer's instructions to fuse traced patterns to wrong side of fabrics. Do not remove paper backing.
3. Use scissors to cut out appliqué pieces along traced lines.

MACHINE PIECING

Precise cutting, followed by accurate piecing, will ensure that all pieces of quilt top fit together well.

• Set sewing machine stitch length for approximately 11 stitches per inch.

• Use neutral-colored general-purpose sewing thread (not quilting thread) in needle and in bobbin.

• An accurate $1/4"$ seam allowance is *essential*. Presser feet that are $1/4"$ wide are available for most sewing machines.

• When piecing, always place pieces right sides together and match raw edges; pin if necessary.

• Chain piecing saves time and will usually result in more accurate piecing.

• Trim away points of seam allowances that extend beyond edges of sewn pieces.

SEWING STRIP SETS

When there are several strips to assemble into a strip set, first sew strips together into pairs, then sew pairs together to form strip set. To help avoid distortion, sew seams in opposite directions *(Fig. 4)*.

Fig. 4

SEWING ACROSS SEAM INTERSECTIONS

When sewing across intersection of two seams, place pieces right sides together and match seams exactly, making sure seam allowances are pressed in opposite directions *(Fig. 5)*.

Fig. 5

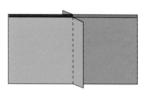

SEWING SHARP POINTS

To ensure sharp points when joining triangular or diagonal pieces, stitch across the center of the "X" (shown in pink) formed on wrong side by previous seams *(Fig. 6)*.

Fig. 6

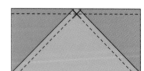

PRESSING

- Use steam iron set on "Cotton" for all pressing.

- Press after sewing each seam.

- Seam allowances are almost always pressed to one side, usually toward darker fabric. However, to reduce bulk it may occasionally be necessary to press seam allowances toward the lighter fabric or even to press them open.

- To prevent dark fabric seam allowance from showing through light fabric, trim darker seam allowance slightly narrower than lighter seam allowance.

- To press long seams, such as those in long strip sets, without curving or other distortion, lay strips across width of the ironing board.

- When sewing blocks into rows, seam allowances may be pressed in one direction in odd numbered rows and in the opposite direction in even numbered rows. When sewing rows together, press seam allowances in one direction.

NEEDLE-TURN APPLIQUÉ

Using needle to turn under seam allowance while blindstitching appliqué to background fabric is called "needle-turn appliqué."

1. Thread a sharps needle with a single strand of general-purpose sewing thread that matches appliqué; knot one end.
2. Begin blindstitching, page 58, on as straight an edge as possible, turning a small section of seam allowance to wrong side with needle, concealing drawn line *(Fig. 7)*.

Fig. 7

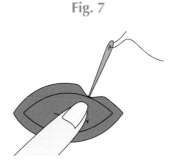

3. To stitch outward points, stitch to ½" from point *(Fig. 8)*. Turn seam allowance under at point *(Fig. 9)*; then turn remainder of seam allowance between stitching and point. Stitch to point, taking two or three stitches at top of point to secure. Turn under small amount of seam allowance past point and resume stitching.

Fig. 8

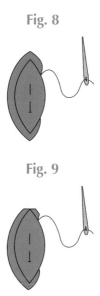

Fig. 9

4. To stitch inward point, stitch to ½" from point *(Fig. 10)*. Clip to but not through seam allowance at point *(Fig. 11)*. Turn seam allowance under between stitching and point. Stitch to point, taking two or three stitches at point to secure. Turn under small amount of seam allowance past point and resume stitching.

Fig. 10

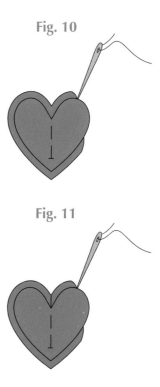

Fig. 11

5. Do not turn under or stitch seam allowances that will be covered by other appliqué pieces.

6. To appliqué pressed bias strips, glue or baste strips in place and blindstitch along edges.

7. To reduce bulk, background fabric behind appliqués may be cut away. After stitching appliqués in place, turn block over and use sharp scissors or specially designed appliqué scissors to trim away background fabric approximately 3/16" from stitching line. Take care not to cut appliqué fabric or stitches.

MAKING A CONTINUOUS BIAS STRIP

1. Cut the **square** called for in the project instructions in half diagonally to make two triangles.

2. With right sides together and using 1/4" seam allowance, sew triangles together *(Fig. 12)*; press seam allowances open.

Fig. 12

3. On wrong side of fabric, draw lines 1" apart *(Fig. 13)*. Cut off any remaining fabric less than this width.

Fig. 13

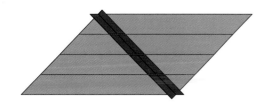

4. With right sides inside, bring short edges together to form a tube; match raw edges so that first drawn line of top section meets second drawn line of bottom section *(Fig. 14)*.

Fig. 14

5. Carefully pin edges together by inserting pins through drawn lines at point where drawn lines intersect, making sure pins go through intersections on both sides. Using 1/4" seam allowance, sew edges together; press seam allowances open.

6. To cut the continuous strip, begin cutting along first drawn line *(Fig. 15)*. Continue cutting along drawn line around tube.

Fig. 15

7. Follow project instructions to use bias strip.

QUILTING

Quilting holds the three layers (top, batting, and backing) of the quilt together and can be done by hand or machine. Because marking, layering, and quilting are interrelated and may be done in different orders depending on circumstances, please read entire Quilting section, pages xxx-xxx, before beginning project.

TYPES OF QUILTING DESIGNS

In the Ditch Quilting
Quilting along seamlines or along edges of appliquéd pieces is called "in the ditch" quilting. This type of quilting should be done on side **opposite** seam allowance and does not have to be marked.

Outline Quilting
Quilting a consistent distance, usually ¼", from seam or appliqué is called "outline" quilting. Outline quilting may be marked, or ¼" masking tape may be placed along seamlines for quilting guide. (Do not leave tape on quilt longer than necessary, since it may leave an adhesive residue.)

Motif Quilting
Quilting a design, such as a feathered wreath, is called "motif" quilting. This type of quilting should be marked before basting quilt layers together.

Echo Quilting
Quilting that follows the outline of an appliquéd or pieced design with two or more parallel lines is called "echo" quilting. This type of quilting does not need to be marked.

Crosshatch Quilting
Quilting straight lines in a grid pattern is called "crosshatch" quilting. Lines may be stitched parallel to edges of quilt or stitched diagonally. This type of quilting may be marked or stitched using a guide.

Meandering Quilting
Quilting in random curved lines and swirls is called "meandering" quilting. Quilting lines should not cross or touch each other. This type of quilting does not need to be marked.

Stipple Quilting
Closely spaced meandering quilting is called "stipple" quilting. Stippling will flatten the quilt and is often stitched in background areas to raise appliquéd or pieced designs. This type of quilting does not need to be marked.

MARKING QUILTING LINES
Quilting lines may be marked using fabric marking pencils, chalk markers, or water- or air-soluble pens.

Simple quilting designs may be marked with chalk or chalk pencil after basting. A small area may be marked, then quilted, before moving to next area to be marked. Intricate designs should be marked before basting using a more durable marker.

Caution: Pressing may permanently set some marks. **Test** different markers **on scrap fabric** to find one that marks clearly and can be thoroughly removed.

A wide variety of pre-cut quilting stencils, as well as entire books of quilting patterns, are available. Using a stencil makes it easier to mark intricate or repetitive designs.

To make a stencil from a pattern, center template plastic over pattern and use a permanent marker to trace pattern onto plastic. Use a craft knife with single or double blade to cut channels along traced lines *(Fig. 16)*.

Fig. 16

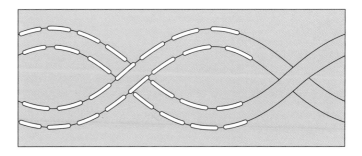

PREPARING THE BACKING

To allow for slight shifting of quilt top during quilting, backing should be approximately 4" larger on all sides. Yardage requirements listed for quilt backings are calculated for 43"/44"w fabric. Using 90"w or 108"w fabric for the backing may eliminate piecing and use less yardage. To piece a backing using 43"/44"w fabric, use the following instructions.

1. Measure length and width of quilt top; add 8" to each measurement.
2. Cut backing fabric into two lengths slightly longer than determined *length* measurement. Trim selvages. Place lengths with right sides facing and sew long edges together, forming tube *(Fig. 17)*. Match seams and press along one fold *(Fig. 18)*. Cut along pressed fold to form single piece *(Fig. 19)*.

Fig. 17   Fig. 18

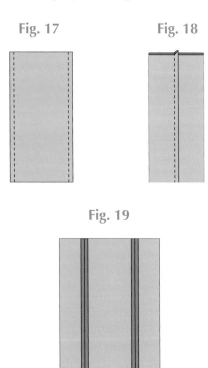

Fig. 19

3. Trim backing to size determined in Step 1; press seam allowances open.

CHOOSING THE BATTING

The appropriate batting will make quilting easier. For fine hand quilting, choose low-loft batting. All cotton or cotton/polyester blend battings work well for machine quilting because the cotton helps "grip" quilt layers. If quilt is to be tied, a high-loft batting, sometimes called extra-loft or fat batting, may be used to make quilt "fluffy."

Types of batting include cotton, polyester, wool, cotton/polyester blend, cotton/wool blend, and silk.

When selecting batting, refer to package labels for characteristics and care instructions. Cut batting same size as prepared backing.

ASSEMBLING THE QUILT

1. Examine wrong side of quilt top closely; trim any seam allowances and clip any threads that may show through front of the quilt. Press quilt top, being careful not to "set" any marked quilting lines.
2. Place backing **wrong** side up on flat surface. Use masking tape to tape edges of backing to surface. Place batting on top of backing fabric. Smooth batting gently, being careful not to stretch or tear. Center quilt top **right** side up on batting.
3. Use 1" rustproof safety pins to "pin-baste" all layers together, spacing pins approximately 4" apart. Begin at center and work toward outer edges to secure all layers. If possible, place pins away from areas that will be quilted, although pins may be removed as needed when quilting.

MACHINE QUILTING METHODS

Use general-purpose thread in bobbin. Do not use quilting thread. Thread the needle of machine with general-purpose thread or transparent monofilament thread to make quilting blend with quilt top fabrics. Use decorative thread, such as a metallic or contrasting-color general-purpose thread, to make quilting lines stand out more.

Straight-Line Quilting

The term "straight-line" is somewhat deceptive, since curves (especially gentle ones) as well as straight lines can be stitched with this technique.

1. Set stitch length for six to ten stitches per inch and attach a walking foot to sewing machine.
2. Determine which section of quilt will have the longest continuous quilting line, oftentimes the area from center top to center bottom. Roll up and secure each edge of the quilt to help reduce the bulk, keeping fabrics smooth. Smaller projects may not need to be rolled.
3. Begin stitching on longest quilting line, using very short stitches for the first $1/4$" to "lock" quilting. Stitch across project, using one hand on each side of walking foot to slightly spread fabric and to guide fabric through machine. Lock stitches at end of quilting line.
4. Continue machine quilting, stitching longer quilting lines first to stabilize quilt before moving on to other areas.

Free-Motion Quilting

Free-motion quilting may be free form or may follow a marked pattern.

1. Attach a darning foot to sewing machine and lower or cover feed dogs.
2. Position quilt under darning foot; lower foot. Holding top thread, take a stitch and pull bobbin thread to top of quilt. To "lock" beginning of quilting line, hold top and bobbin threads while making three to five stitches in place.

3. Use one hand on each side of darning foot to slightly spread fabric and to move fabric through the machine. Even stitch length is achieved by using smooth, flowing hand motion and steady machine speed. Slow machine speed and fast hand movement will create long stitches. Fast machine speed and slow hand movement will create short stitches. Move quilt sideways, back and forth, in a circular motion, or in a random motion to create desired designs; do not rotate quilt. Lock stitches at end of each quilting line.

ADDING A HANGING SLEEVE

Attaching a hanging sleeve to back of wall hanging or quilt before the binding is added allows a project to be displayed on a wall.

1. Measure width of quilt top edge and subtract 1". Cut piece of fabric 7"w by determined measurement.
2. Press short edges of fabric piece $1/4$" to wrong side; press edges $1/4$" to wrong side again and machine stitch in place.
3. Matching wrong sides, fold piece in half lengthwise to form tube.
4. Follow project instructions to sew binding to quilt top and to trim backing and batting. Before Blindstitching binding to backing, match raw edges and stitch hanging sleeve to center top edge on back of quilt.
5. Finish binding quilt, treating hanging sleeve as part of backing.
6. Blindstitch bottom of hanging sleeve to backing, taking care not to stitch through to front of quilt.

BINDING

Binding encloses the raw edges of quilt. Binding may be cut from straight lengthwise or crosswise grain of fabric. Strips may be pieced to achieve necessary length.

1. Use diagonal seams *(Fig. 20)* to sew **binding strips** together end-to-end.

Fig. 20

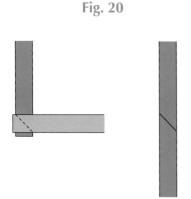

2. Matching wrong sides and raw edges, press strip(s) in half lengthwise to complete binding.
3. Beginning with one end near center on bottom edge of quilt, lay binding around quilt to make sure that seams in binding will not end up at a corner. Adjust placement if necessary. Matching raw edges of binding to raw edge of quilt top, pin binding to right side of quilt along one edge.
4. When you reach first corner, mark $1/4$" from corner of quilt top *(Fig. 21)*.

Fig. 21

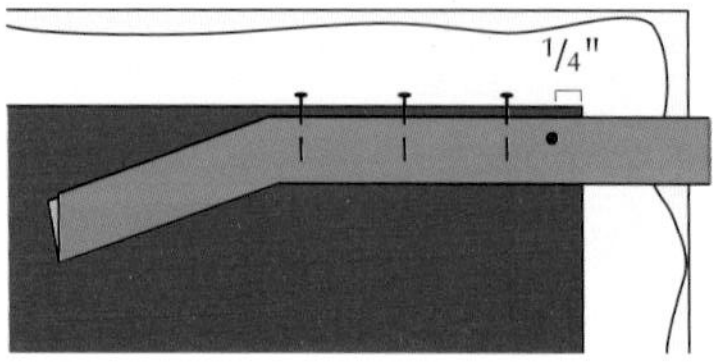

5. Beginning approximately 10" from end of binding and using $1/4$" seam allowance, sew binding to quilt, backstitching at beginning of stitching and at mark *(Fig. 22)*. Lift needle out of fabric and clip thread.

Fig. 22

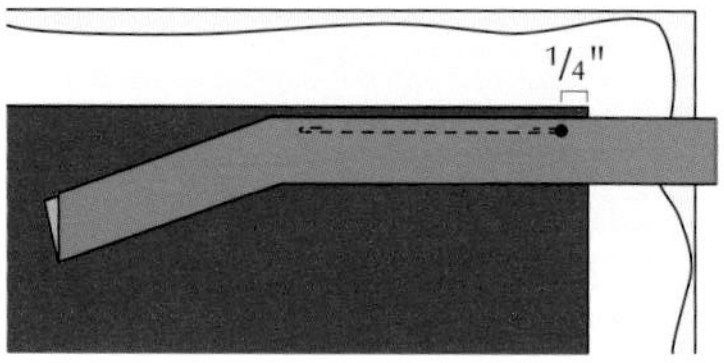

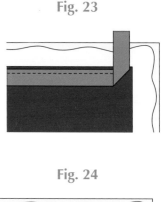

6. Fold binding as shown in *Figs. 23-24* and pin binding to adjacent side, matching raw edges. When you've reached the next corner, mark $1/4$" from the edge of quilt top.

Fig. 23

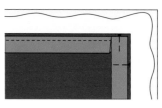

Fig. 24

7. Backstitching at edge of quilt top, sew pinned binding to quilt *(Fig. 25)*; backstitch at the next mark. Lift needle out of fabric and clip thread.

Fig. 25

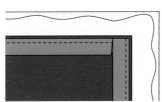

8. Continue sewing binding to quilt, stopping approximately 10" from starting point *(Fig. 26)*.

Fig. 26

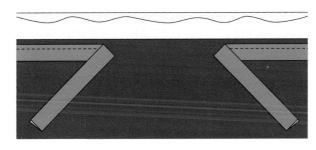

9. Bring beginning and end of binding to center of opening and fold each end back, leaving a ¹⁄₄" space between folds *(Fig. 27)*. Finger press folds.

Fig. 27

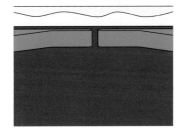

10. Unfold ends of binding and draw a line across wrong side in finger-pressed crease. Draw a line through the lengthwise pressed fold of binding at the same spot to create a cross mark. With edge of ruler at cross mark, line up 45° angle marking on ruler with one long side of binding. Draw a diagonal line from edge to edge. Repeat on remaining end, making sure that the two diagonal lines are angled the same way *(Fig. 28)*.

Fig. 28

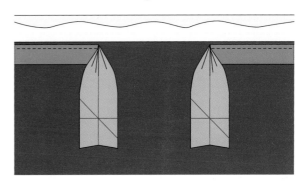

11. Matching right sides and diagonal lines, pin binding ends together at right angles *(Fig. 29)*.

Fig. 29

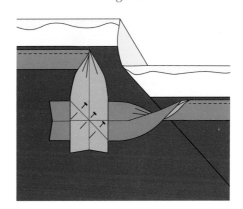

12. Machine stitch along diagonal line *(Fig. 30)*, removing pins as you stitch.

Fig. 30

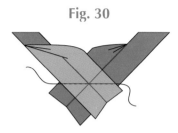

13. Lay binding against quilt to double check that it is correct length.

14. Trim binding ends, leaving ¼" seam allowance; press seam open. Stitch binding to quilt.

15. Trim backing and batting even with edges of quilt top.

16. On one edge of quilt, fold binding over to quilt backing and pin pressed edge in place, covering stitching line *(Fig. 31)*. On adjacent side, fold binding over, forming a mitered corner *(Fig. 32)*. Repeat to pin remainder of binding in place.

Fig. 31

Fig. 32

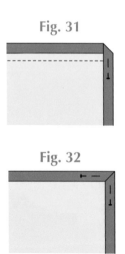

17. Blindstitch binding to backing, taking care not to stitch through to front of quilt.

BLIND STITCH

Come up at 1, go down at 2, and come up at 3 *(Fig. 33)*. Length of stitches may be varied as desired.

Fig. 33

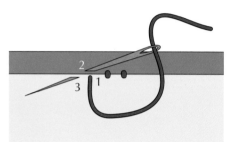

SIGNING AND DATING YOUR QUILT

A completed quilt is a work of art and should be signed and dated. There are many different ways to do this and numerous books on the subject. The label should reflect the style of the quilt, the occasion or person for which it was made, and the quilter's own particular talents. Following are suggestions for recording the history of quilt or adding a sentiment for future generations.

- Embroider quilter's name, date, and any additional information on the quilt top or backing. Matching floss, such as cream floss on a white border, will leave a subtle record. Bright or contrasting floss will make the information stand out.

- Make a label from muslin and use a permanent marker to write the information. Use different colored permanent markers to make the label more decorative. Stitch the label to the back of the quilt.

- Use photo-transfer paper to add an image to a white or cream fabric label. Stitch the label to the back of the quilt.

- Piece an extra block from the quilt top pattern to use as a label. Add information with permanent fabric pen. Appliqué block to back of quilt.

- Write message on appliquéd design from quilt top. Attach the appliqué to the back of the quilt.

CARING FOR YOUR QUILT

- Wash finished quilt in cold water on gentle cycle with mild soap. Soaps such as Orvus® Paste or Charlie's Soap®, which have no softeners, fragrances, whiteners, or other additives are safest. Rinse twice in cold water.

- Use a dye magnet such as Shout® Color Catcher® each time quilt is washed to absorb any dyes that bleed. When washing a quilt for the first time, you may chose to use two dye magnets for extra caution.

- Dry quilt on low heat/air fluff in 15 minute increments until dry.

THANK YOU!

To Da Gamma Textiles, www.dagama.co.za, for providing many of the lovely fabrics used for the projects in this book.

To Cathie Shoemaker of A Stitch In Time Longarm Machine Quilting, www.astitchintimequilting.com, for the beautiful machine quilting on all the quilts.

To Nancy Busby for her excellent hand appliqué and machine construction of the Christmas Stocking.

Metric Conversion Chart			
Inches x 2.54 = centimeters (cm)		Yards x .9144 = meters (m)	
Inches x 25.4 = millimeters (mm)		Yards x 91.44 = centimeters (cm)	
Inches x .0254 = meters (m)		Centimeters x .3937 = inches (")	
		Meters x 1.0936 = yards (yd)	

Standard Equivalents					
⅛"	3.2 mm	0.32 cm	⅛ yard	11.43 cm	0.11 m
¼"	6.35 mm	0.635 cm	¼ yard	22.86 cm	0.23 m
⅜"	9.5 mm	0.95 cm	⅜ yard	34.29 cm	0.34 m
½"	12.7 mm	1.27 cm	½ yard	45.72 cm	0.46 m
⅝"	15.9 mm	1.59 cm	⅝ yard	57.15 cm	0.57 m
¾"	19.1 mm	1.91 cm	¾ yard	68.58 cm	0.69 m
⅞"	22.2 mm	2.22 cm	⅞ yard	80 cm	0.8 m
1"	25.4 mm	2.54 cm	1 yard	91.44 cm	0.91 m

Holly Hill Quilt Designs evolved through Mary Jane Carey's love of quilting. Coming from a long line of quilters, including the Great-Grandmother whose name she shares, Mary Jane's first quilting endeavor was in 1970. She made a quilt from bed sheets because quilting fabrics were not readily available at that time. In 1995, Mary Jane opened The Christmas Shoppe, selling handmade Santas and quilts she made. Since that time, the quilting side of the business has grown into a full-fledged online shop with fabrics, patterns, books, and notions. Mary Jane also vends at various quilt shows across the US. Mary Jane says, "The love of quilting, and especially quilts with appliqué, have warmed our hearts here at Holly Hill Quilt Designs. We hope they will warm yours, too." Stop by and visit Mary Jane online at www.hollyhillquiltdesigns.com.

Production Team: Technical Editor – Lisa Lancaster; Technical Writer – Jean Lewis; Graphic Artist – Becca Snider Tally, Photography Stylist – Christy Myers, Photographer – Mark Mathews.

We have made every effort to ensure that these instructions are accurate and complete. We cannot, however, be responsible for human error, typographical mistakes, or variations in individual work.